First published in 2021 by Wayland

Wayland, an imprint of Hachette Children's Group
Part of Hodder and Stoughton
Carmelite House
50 Victoria Embankment
London EC4Y 0DZ

An Hachette UK Company
www.hachette.co.uk
www.hachettechildrens.co.uk

Printed and bound in China

Concept design: Sarah Finan
Series design: Paul Cherrill Creative Design
Editor: Victoria Brooker

HB ISBN: 9781526317568
PB ISBN: 9781526317575
EBK ISBN: 9781526317988

I DON'T HAVE ENOUGH

A FIRST LOOK AT POVERTY

Written by
PAT THOMAS

Illustrated by
CLARE KEAY

WAYLAND

Many of us have more than we need.
More food than we can eat, more clothes than
we can wear, lots of different rooms to live and play
in and more toys than we have time to play with.

But there are people all around us who don't have enough of all these things.

Not having enough is sometimes described as being poor, or living in poverty.

Poverty is when you don't have enough money or support to help you with basic human needs, such as food, shelter, medicine or clothing.

People living in poverty
often need help – from their
families, friends, communities
and governments in order to survive.

But sometimes help can be hard to get.

WHAT ABOUT YOU?

Do you know what it feels like not to have enough? What are some of the ways we help people living in poverty?

Some people think if others are poor, it's their own fault for not working hard enough.

But what if that's not true?

What if the place where they worked closed down? Or they are sick or have a disability that makes it hard to work or find a job?

What if they are elderly, or alone, or were denied a chance because of the colour of their skin?

What if they had to leave where they were living because it wasn't safe anymore?

These things happen to people every day.
They happen in faraway places and they
happen in places very near to us.

And when these things happen, people are left without jobs and homes. Families and friendships can break up.

Being poor can make people
feel like nobody cares, like
they don't matter and
like they are not
good enough.

Parents can feel stressed and seem angry because they can't give their families the things they need.

Children can feel sad and scared. They may feel too hungry to do their homework or join in activities or sports.

When you are poor, there may not be money for medicine if you get sick. You may have to walk places because there's no money for a car or the bus. If something gets broken, you may not be able to replace it.

Parents may not be able to afford presents or treats for their families. They may have to sell or give up things they own in order to pay a bill or buy food.

WHAT ABOUT YOU?

Do you know the difference between want and need? Can you name some things that we all need money for? If you had to give up some of those things in order to buy food, what would you give up?

Being poor doesn't always mean being out of work. Some people living in poverty may even have more than one job.

But they get paid so little that they still don't have enough.

Many people living in poverty also work in jobs that can easily be taken away, and where there is hardly any chance of earning more money.

When people don't have enough
money, they may have to
move out of their
homes.

They might go to a shelter or emergency housing
where families have to all share one small room.

Usually they can't stay long in these places, so they may move around a lot.

Some people may have no choice but to live in their cars or on the street.

People who are poor may not like to talk about it. They may feel embarrassed that others might see how little they have. They may worry that they will be bullied or made fun of.

That can mean that a lot
of the poverty around us
is hidden.

But a lot of
it isn't.

WHAT ABOUT YOU?

In what ways does being poor make a person
different? What do you think would be the
hardest part of not having a home of your own?

We all want to live in a world where there is no poverty and everyone has what they need to be healthy and happy.

One person can't make all the poverty in the world go away. But one person can make a difference to other people, in their community and in other parts of the world.

We can all show kindness
and respect to others.
We can offer help.
We can share what
we have a lot of with
those who have
hardly anything.

If we all learn to
share, then more
of us will have
enough.

HOW TO USE THIS BOOK

Poverty is a complex and emotive subject. It can take a long time to talk through all there is to say about it. This book is aimed at helping to open up first discussions with young children and is meant to be read with children as a way of encouraging them to be active partners in the discussion. Try reading the book first and familiarising yourself with its content before you begin. The "What about you?" questions throughout the text can be useful prompts for understanding things from your child's point of view. You may find benefit in reading the book with your child more than once. Repetition allows your child to formulate thoughts and questions as the need arises.

Start with the familiar. With young children who are still very 'me' focused, concrete discussions about someone you know, or someone you have seen, who is struggling with poverty may be more productive than more abstract discussions about invisible 'others' in faraway places.

Be prepared for questions. Research suggests that by the time children enter preschool they are aware of differences between the rich and the poor. When children start asking questions, it's a sign that they are ready to learn more. Before you begin to talk to your child about poverty consider your own beliefs and what you want to say. Think also about the things you do or don't do in relation to poverty. If, for instance, you have a policy of not giving money to people in the street, explain why. Make sure you are prepared to answer any questions that come up in an age-appropriate way.

Talk about feelings. There are lots of practical impacts that poverty has on people's lives, but there are also emotional impacts. Adults and children living in poverty can feel more stressed and unhappy, left out, or more alone than others. Helping children to understand its emotional impacts as well can make the issue more 'real' for them, as well as help humanise the subject and encourage empathy.

Provide reassurance. Talking about poverty may cause some children to feel anxious about whether their family might run out of food or be homeless someday. Talk about any safeguards you might have in place such as a relative who can help. Explain that there are government programs in place that help people who are in need. As an adult, you know that even the best safeguards are not foolproof, but children need reassurance. Explain also that there is a difference between not having the money to buy everything you want and being truly poor.

Avoid value judgements. We all have to grapple with what we think is right or wrong, good or bad and who we think is to blame. But with complex topics it is easy to be quick to jump to conclusions, or be overly rigid or critical in our assessments of others. These habits can prevent us from understanding where other people are coming from and can be associated with intolerance and prejudice. Encourage tolerance in your child and help them to understand that poverty does not define a person and there is no single experience of poverty or culture of poverty.

Schools can help. Lessons can tackle practical issues, such as looking at how poverty manifests in the local community as well as in the wider world. They can also challenge preconceptions and beliefs, and reinforce the idea that a person living in poverty does not need to be saved, they need to be helped.

Asking the class to vote true or false by a show of hands on a number of different statements around poverty is a good way to gauge what their level of knowledge is. From there, age-appropriate lessons can explore prejudices about poverty, the difference between short- and long-term poverty and ways to help those in poverty, as well as an understanding of the vocabulary around poverty, such as inequality, community, charity, fairness, justice and discrimination.

Schools can also involve children of all ages in helping the community, for instance, through drives to donate food, toys and clothing to those in need. These provide great teaching moments around sharing and helping and a chance for children to feel as if they are part of a caring community.

Schools must also tackle the issue of poverty institutionally. Does your school assign work requiring computer and internet access or other costly resources? Can it provide materials and in-school time for this work to be completed? Does your school keep stocks of essentials, such as school supplies, snacks and clothes, for students who may need them? Does it have a programme to supplement those who cannot afford school trips?

FURTHER READING

A Shelter in Our Car
Monica Gunning (Children's Book Press, 2013)

It's a No-Money Day
Kate Milner (Barrington Stoke, 2019)

Last Stop on Market Street
Matt de la Peña (Puffin, 2017)

Poverty and Hunger (Children in Our World)
Louise Spilsbury (Wayland, 2018)

Those Shoes
Maribeth Boelts (Candlewick Press, 2016)

Yard Sale
Eve Bunting (Candlewick Press, 2015)

Still a Family: A Story of Homelessness
Brenda Reeves Sturgis (Albert Whitman & Company, 2018)

USEFUL WEBSITES

Teaching Tolerance
www.tolerance.org

Issues Online
www.issuesonline.co.uk

Child Poverty Action Group
www.cpag.org.uk

The Children's Society
www.childrenssociety.org.uk